By
Moriah Elizabeth
AND _____

(your name here)

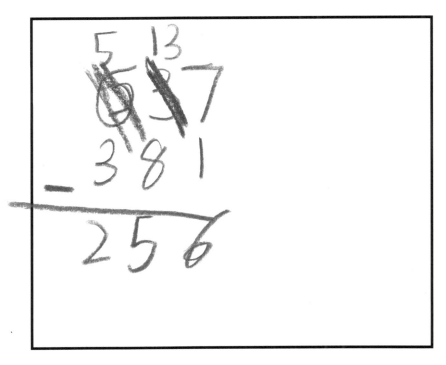

EMPTY BOX
(FILL HOWEVER YOU SEE FIT)

ISBN−13:978-0692452745

ISBN−10: 0692452745

YOU MAY ENJOY THIS BOOK IF...

you are creative, would like to become more creative, enjoy doodling, enjoy journaling, are an art lover, want to have fun, are bored, are uninspired or are unsure of which one of these you are!

ABOUT THIS BOOK:

Each page in this book includes a prompt to inspire creativity. The goal is to turn this book into something completely unique AND to have a blast doing it!

Be *Original*

Make. Each. Page. Special.

challenge yourself

embrace accidents/mistakes

Be *Adventurous*

don't be afraid to get messy

NEVER doubt yourself

HAVE FUN!

DECORATING THE FRONT/BACK COVER:

When it comes to decorating the cover, be careful with the types of media you are using to prevent smudging and splotching.

BEST MATERIALS TO USE:

–Permanent Markers
  (let dry completely before touching to avoid smudging)

–Acrylic Paint

–Other Decorating Materials
  (stickers, gems, scrapbook paper, decorative tape, etc.)

MIXED RESULTS:

–Colored Pencils
  (some brands may not be pigmented enough for even coverage)

–Crayons
  (apply easily, but may produce splotchy color)

MATERIALS TO AVOID:

–Washable Markers
  (prone to smudging)

–Felt Tip Pens
  (prone to smudging)

–Watercolor Paint
  (will not adhere properly)

DECORATING THE INTERIOR:

The pages in this book are a little thin, but we can work around that (after all, we all are creative people here!).

 BEST MATERIALS TO USE:

−Pens

−Acrylic Paint

−Pencils & Colored Pencils

−Crayons

−Chalk & Charcoal

−Other Decorating Materials
   (stickers, gems, scrapbook paper, decorative tape, etc.)

TO USE WET MEDIA (markers, watercolor paint, etc.)

If you want to use wet media on certain pages, no problem! To prevent bleeding through the paper, use wet media on a separate piece of paper and glue your finished artwork into the book. OR glue a blank sheet of paper into the book first, trim the edges, and then create on top. **You can even cut a window in the paper so you can still see the directions.**

PROTECT YOUR ARTWORK!

To preserve your artwork and keep it neat, try applying a matte clear coat over top, or use clear packing tape to cover your art.

To see a video tutorial of these TIPS & TRICKS, check out Moriah Elizabeth's Create This Book 2 introduction video on YouTube.

to begin
CREATE
THIS BOOK

(fill in the stars as you complete each task)

Customize the front cover
(add stickers, tape, drawings, writing etc.)

**Add color and/or text to the spine and
edges of the book**

**Make the title and copyright page
more interesting**

Add a personal touch to this page
(doodles, a decorative border etc.)

CREATE A Fancy Name

Write your name on this page in a fancy way.

Ideas: Use large text, write with your best pen, include your favorite color etc.

CREATE A RULE

Make a rule for yourself and follow it on each page of this book (unless it conflicts with the instructions). Write your rule in the box provided.

Examples: draw a symbol on every page, date the bottom of each page, add a sticker to each page, etc.

RULE BOX ↓

Create A Monochrome

choose
ONE
COLOR

Use **only** that color
to decorate this page.

CREATE THE FOLLOWING Lists:

THINGS
YOU
LIKE:

THINGS
YOU
DISLIKE:

CREATE
a *music* inspired page

Turn on some music.
Let the music inspire your decorations.

CREATE
A PAGE
OF GARBAGE

Draw, photograph, write, or attach a bunch of items that you regularly throw in the garbage.

# CREATE A PET

Make this page into a pet.
Don't forget to give it a name!

CREATE
A PAGE OF POLKA DOTS

PUT POLKA DOTS ON THIS PAGE.

Create A RECORDED CONVERSATION

Sit in a room with other people.
Write down everything you hear.

CREATE AN ARRAY OF MEDIA

Draw one object over and over, using a different medium each time (one drawing with marker, one with pen, one with pencil etc.).

NOTE: If you are feeling extra adventurous, try using unconventional media like ketchup, chocolate, mud or anything else you can think of!

CREATE **FOLDS**

Fold this page any way you want!

create
LETTERS

Fill this page with letters.
Use them for aesthetic value
rather than writing words.

CREATE A MEAL

Draw/write about
your ideal meal.
Don't forget dessert!

CREATE

SIMPLISTIC DRAWINGS

Fill this page with stick
figure drawings.

CREATE A
Family

Draw, attach, or
assemble an image
of a family.

CREATE A

Draw or put together some sort of

BORDER

interesting border around these pages.

CREATE AN
Unusual Combo

**Think of an object.
Draw it as if made of
an unusual material.**

Examples: a ceiling fan
made out of donuts,
a car made of flowers

CREATE A RECORD OF YOUR WEEK

Answer each of the following questions everyday for a week

1.) What did you wear?

Mon. _____
Tues. _____
Wed. _____
Thur. _____
Fri. _____
Sat. _____
Sun. _____

2.) What did you eat?

Mon. _____
Tues. _____
Wed. _____
Thur. _____
Fri. _____
Sat. _____
Sun. _____

3.) What was the BEST part of the day?

Mon. _____

Tues. _____

Wed. _____

Thur. _____

Fri. _____

Sat. _____

Sun. _____

4.) What was the WORST part of the day?

Mon. _____

Tues. _____

Wed. _____

Thur. _____

Fri. _____

Sat. _____

Sun. _____

5.) What was one random activity you did?

Mon. _____

Tues. _____

Wed. _____

Thur. _____

Fri. _____

Sat. _____

Sun. _____

Create *Quick Sketches*

Draw something in ONE minute or less.
Repeat, drawing different things each time.

01:00

Create a **GROWTH** chart

Figure out a way to show some kind of growing process.

CREATE A COLLECTION

Start a collection.
Document it here.

Draw it.
Photograph it.
Or attach it to the page.

CREATE A REFUSAL

Choose one page's instructions in this book to ignore.
Indicate your refusal by cutting out the
"INSTRUCTIONS VOID" box and attaching it to the
page that you wish to refuse.

Draw your symbol of refusal in the box below:

INSTRUCTIONS VOID

CREATE A BUMPY PAGE

Lay this page over a textured or bumpy surface.
Try to write or draw something.

CREATE A PAGE OF STRIPES

Draw stripes on this page.

CREATE *a Signature*

Use the lines below to practice your signature. Try to include some variation. Star the one you think is best.

_____

(SIGN HERE)

_____

(SIGN HERE)

_____

(SIGN HERE)

_____

(SIGN HERE)

_____

(SIGN HERE)

_____

(SIGN HERE)

_____

(SIGN HERE)

_____

(SIGN HERE)

_____

(SIGN HERE)

_____

(SIGN HERE)

_____

(SIGN HERE)

_____

(SIGN HERE)

_____

(SIGN HERE)

CREATE ART WITH **WAX**

Decorate this page using only wax
(candle wax, crayons etc.).

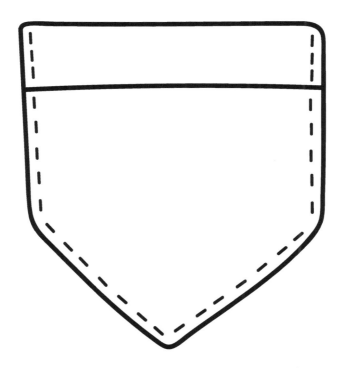

CREATE A POCKET

Apply glue inside the dotted lines on page 57. Be careful not to glue the top! Close the book and allow the glue to dry.

Store something in the pocket that is created between the two pages.

CREATE AN *inkblot*

Drop ink, paint or any other colored fluid onto this page. Make observations about it.

CREATE
A PAGE FOR STICKERS

Place stickers all
over this page.

CREATE → DIRECTIONS

Add your own directions for this page.
Write your prompt in the box below.

CREATE A

SECRET
SECRET

Write a secret here.
Cover it up somehow.

CREATE obscure shapes
FILL this page with unusual shapes.

RULE: Do not add anything recognizable to this page (make it purely abstract).

CREATE BOREDOM
Make this page boring.

CREATE DOODLES

Fill this entire page with mindless doodling.

CREATE A
Fantasy Home

Design a home in _____

(Fill with fantasy location)

"create" A PAGE OF QUOTES

Fill this page with inspirational quotes.

CREATE A **FABRIC** PAGE

Attach a piece of fabric (or bits of fabric) to this page.

CREATE AN ALIEN

Draw what you imagine an alien looks like.
Try to think outside the box!

CREATE A CHALLENGE

Fill in this page without using your
hands in any way.

CREATE A LIST OF FADS

Write, Illustrate or place pictures
of anything that is trending at the moment.

Create
EMBARRASSMENT

Capture embarrassment on this page.

CREATE A PAGE OF CHECKERS

Put checkers here.

CREATE A

SHARED DRAWING

Start a drawing on this page.
Have a friend finish it.

CREATE
PLANS FOR A BUILDING

Draft up some plans for some
sort of building or structure.

create color
combinations

Play around with different color combinations.
Group colors to see how they look together.
Make note of your favorites.

CREATE A PROGRESSION

Draw something simple. Add to it.
Keep adding until you can no longer
distinguish the original drawing.

Create Nostalgia

Make this page sentimental.

create an
ADVERTISEMENT

Draw an AD for a product
(real or made up).

Create
Instructions

Write up detailed instructions for a very simple, everyday task. Include diagrams if necessary.

Examples: How to eat a bowl of cereal, how to make the bed

CREATE NONSENSICAL
CREATURES

Draw or assemble made up creatures.
Draw them from imagination or use bits
or magazine photos to invent your own
creatures. Be sure to name them!

create your
Favorite

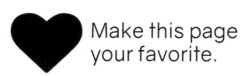

Make this page
your favorite.

create your
Least Favorite

Make this page
your least favorite.

Create a Page
OF EMOTION

Write about, draw, or attach pictures of at least three different emotions here.

CREATE STENCILS

Cut shapes out of this page. Use the cut outs as stencils on the next page (pg. 113).

PAGE FOR STENCILED SHAPES

CREATE A PAIR.
DRAW A SET
OF TWINS.

CREATE STRAIGHT LINES

Make a design
using only straight lines.

CREATE WEATHER-BASED DECOR

Fill this page based on the current weather condition.

DATE:___/___/____

CREATE DRAWING VARIATION

Choose one object. Draw it over and over again using as many different methods as possible (eyes closed, while jumping etc.). The more bizarre, the better! Record whatever method you used next to each drawing.

CREATE A
PERSON

Come up with a character.
Draw what they look like.
Describe their personality.
List their likes and dislikes.

create smudges

Coat your fingers with ink, paint or charcoal.
Smear the color across the page.

Create an Interview

Make a list of questions to ask a friend or
family member and record their responses here.

Create an Outfit

Draw or attach a picture of your favorite outfit. Use either an outfit you own, or one you would like to own.

**Be sure to explain why you love it so much
(comfort, style, color etc.).**

CREATE A **SWITCH**

Come up with an idea for this page.

Switch up the plan about halfway through completing your original idea.

Don't plan your second idea until you have already started your first one.

CREATE *a Fan Page*

Choose a favorite movie or TV show. Fill this
page with notes, pictures, characters or
quotes from the film/show.

CREATE A SYMBOL

Come up with an original symbol.

Draw it here. Write about what it means.

Create Without Thinking

Do something to this page
without thinking.

**Do it quickly.
Do not plan.**

CREATE A PAINT-BY-NUMBER

Choose a set of colors. Assign each color a number. Label each part of the image with the number that corresponds to the color that should be used in that area. Color it in or have a friend fill it in for you.

CREATE A COLLAGE

Collect paper scraps or pictures and glue

them all over these two pages.

CREATE A FLAW

Draw, write or design something here.
Insert an **OBVIOUS** flaw.

Create an Adventure

Go for a walk (outside or indoors).

Document your adventure.

CREATE A PAGE OF
Notes

Take notes on something
mundane (people around you,
the weather, what the room
looks like etc.).

CREATE A
PROFESSION

Come up with a ridiculous job that you know is nonexistent. Write about it/draw pictures of it here.

CREATE **A TEST**

Test the difference between your right and left hand.

Draw/write something in box #1 with your dominant hand.

BOX #1

Try to duplicate your writing/drawing in box #2 using your non-dominant hand.

BOX #2

CREATE A PLAYLIST

Think of songs that are special to you. Write down a few song titles and what they mean to you.

CREATE A
CONTRADICTION

Make up something contradictory
(hot ice, bright darkness). Draw or
write about it here.

CREATE A **CONTOUR DRAWING**

Draw something without lifting up your pencil.

← Contour Shoe

CREATE
PATTERNS
Fill this page with patterns.

CREATE
a dialogue

Write a conversation between two or more people. Try writing something short and simple if you get stuck on ideas.

CREATE AN
EMPTY SETTING

Draw some sort setting (city, beach, mountains).
Leave it empty (no people or animals).

Create an
Arrangement
of Doodles

Doodle or write in a variety of places.
Collect the scraps and attach them here
(napkins from restaurants, notes from school).

Create Color Dispute

Draw a picture using all the "wrong" colors
(example: purple grass, a pink tree).

CREATE
A Dedication

Dedicate this page to something. Write about
it/draw it/attach pictures of it here.

I _____ Dedicate this page to:
(YOUR NAME)

_____
(SUBJECT OF DEDICATION)

CREATE

SOMETHING EDUCATIONAL

Center this page around something
 you learned in school.

CREATE A

PHYSICAL COLLECTION OF SPECIFIC OBJECTS

Choose one of the following objects to collect on this page: buttons, feathers, string OR wrappers.

CREATE a page for your
Favorite Character

Choose one of your favorite cartoon characters.
Draw him or her on this page.

CREATE A PAGE FROM THE PAST

Attach something from the past here (photos, documents, old drawings, etc.)

CREATE
Unlikely Art

Make art out of ordinary subjects
(household objects, numbers, logos).

CREATE CHAOS

Figure out a way to make this page appear chaotic (jumbled, messy, disorderly).

create **CUTS** through layers

Cut shapes through several pages in a magazine or newspaper at once. Glue the pieces here.

CREATE A COMBO

Choose two of your favorite people, animals
or objects. Combine them.

CREATE A WALL

Pretend this page is a wall.

Add graffiti to it.

CREATE **TIMED** DECORATION

Use a timer to decorate this page in exactly 10 minutes. No more, no less.

CREATE
AN UNUSUAL
SUPER POWER

Come up with an original superhero. Give him or her an unusual super power.

Create Textures

Fill this page with a variety of different textures.

CREATE UGLINESS.

Make this page ugly.

CREATE
A PAGE FOR A PET

Dedicate this page to a pet (if you don't have
a pet, use a friend's pet or one from TV.).

create an
APPLIED SUGGESTION

Ask a friend what you should do on this
page. Use their FIRST suggestion.

_____

_____

(WRITE SUGGESTION HERE)

Create
Something
out of
NOTHING

Draw random scribbles on this page.
Make something out of them.

CREATE A RECEIPT

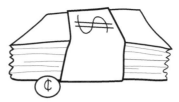

Record everything you buy for a chosen period (a week, a month).

CREATE *a Nature Page*

Make this into a "nature page" by adding any elements of nature that you think necessary.

CREATE

A DIFFERENT DRAWING

Try drawing something
you have never drawn
before. Choose
something random.
Have fun
with it!

CREATE A FOOD PAGE
Decorate this page with food.

CREATE A
COLORLESS PAGE

Decorate this page
without using color.

CREATE A
WINDOW

Put an image of any kind onto the next
page (pg. 213). Cut a window into this
page to reveal the image.

PAGE OUTSIDE THE WINDOW

CREATE AN UPSIDE DOWN PAGE

**Write or draw something on this page
while the book is upside down.**

CREATE BLIND ARTWORK
Do a painting or drawing while closing your eyes.

Create a *Scrapbook* Page

Make a one-page scrapbook. Attach
photos and decorate the page with colored
paper, tape, stickers etc.

CREATE CONTRAST

Think of a pair of opposites.
Present them together on this page.

Examples: good and evil, light and dark etc.

CREATE
AN ASSESSMENT

Dedicated this page to an everyday task.
Write about whether you like or dislike it.

Create Scenery

Think about a place you would like to travel
(real or fantasy). Draw pictures/take notes
about how it would look and feel.

CREATE an *Ending*

Make this page into your official ending of the book. Add a completion date, write about what you got out of the book etc.

Made in the USA
Las Vegas, NV
20 October 2020